Ancient Greece

by
John H. Artman

illustrated by Susan Kropa

Cover by Vanessa Filkins

Copyright © Good Apple, 1991

ISBN No. 0-86653-583-7

Good Apple
A Division of Frank Schaffer Publications, Inc.
23740 Hawthorne Boulevard
Torrance, CA 90505-5927

Table of Contents

GA1310

Time Line for Ancient Greece

Listed below are eighteen important dates for events that took place during the time of the Greeks of the Classical Age. Use these dates and the information provided for each one to fill in the time line on the following page. If you wish, add other dates and information as you study the Greeks.

2200 B.C.	Greek-speaking people arrive in Attica.
1200 B.C.	Dorians invade Greece and destroy the Mycenaean civilization. Athens alone holds out.
750-700 B.C.	Homer writes *Iliad* and *Odyssey*.
700 B.C.	The towns of Attica are combined with Athens to become one political unit.
621 B.C.	Draco revises the Athenian laws.
507 B.C.	Cleisthenes restores Athenian democracy.
490 B.C.	The Persian invasion of mainland Greece is repelled at Marathon.
484 B.C.	Aeschylus wins his first Athenian drama festival.
480 B.C.	Spartans are destroyed at Thermopylae; the Athenian fleet defeats the Persians at Salamis.
455 B.C.	Euripides' first tragedy is performed.
448 B.C.	Athenian Empire is established.
431 B.C.	The Peloponnesian War starts.
429 B.C.	Sophocles' *Oedipus Rex* is produced.
404 B.C.	Athens is totally defeated by Sparta.
399 B.C.	Socrates is condemned to death.
336 B.C.	Philip II of Macedonia is assassinated. Alexander succeeds him.
334 B.C.	Invasion of Persia by Alexander the Great.
323 B.C.	Alexander dies in Babylon.

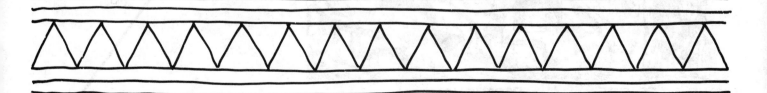

GA1310

Time Line for Ancient Greece

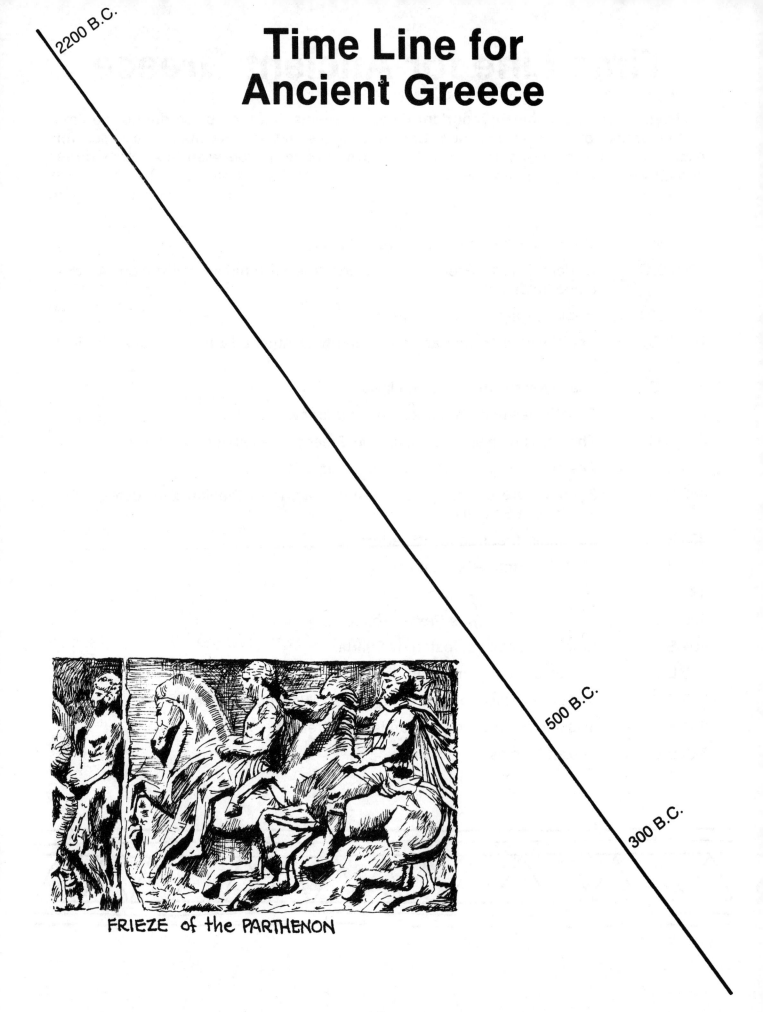

2200 B.C.

500 B.C.

300 B.C.

FRIEZE of the PARTHENON

GA1310

Introduction

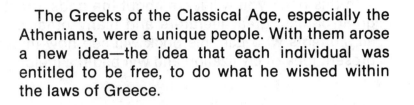

EPIK H
PERICLES

The Greeks of the Classical Age, especially the Athenians, were a unique people. With them arose a new idea—the idea that each individual was entitled to be free, to do what he wished within the laws of Greece.

This was a revolutionary idea in the ancient world. Before the Greeks, there had been the empires of the East—Egyptian, Babylonian, Assyrian, Persian—who believed that man was less than nothing. These civilizations had man groveling before monarchs and deities.

This idea of freedom arose in Greece because every district was separated by mountains or the sea so the people of each district grew up as a distinct group. There were no great river lands like the Nile or the Tigris-Euphrates where it was easy to control a large population under one ruler.

Believing in the worth of the individual, the Classical Greeks, mainly the Athenians, also felt each individual should do his very best at any task he undertook. This came from their idea of excellence. They believed in balance—developing both the mind and the body. This was excellence as they saw it. So anything they did had to be done at their highest abilities. Many Greeks were skilled in several fields. They thought a man could function well as an artist, a soldier, a poet, an athlete or as anything else he undertook.

The Athenians carried this idea out in their great sculpture, their architecture, their magnificent literature, their politics and warfare. They gave western man most of his literary forms, the beginnings of the various schools of philosophy and the sacred trust of freedom for each individual.

But along with this idea of excellence, the Athenians didn't go completely out of control by attempting to be the very best at anything they undertook.

They followed two concepts that were inscribed on the great shrine of Delphi. These two statements were "Nothing in excess" and "Know thyself."

1

GA1310

Using these two concepts to guide them, the Greeks practiced excellence with moderation and each person attempted to learn what he as an individual was capable of.

In this book you will learn about the gods, great heroes, Athens and Sparta, customs, great battles, great literature and many other aspects of Classical Greece. Hopefully, all students who use this book will see how important the ancient Greeks were to our present idea of civilization and will begin a lifelong interest in that great time.

2

GA1310

Greek Gods and Goddesses

The Greeks believed that in the beginning of the earth there was a huge void called Chaos. From this void, eventually, came the Titans led by Chronos. Zeus, the son of Chronos, was the leader of the next race of gods—the Olympians. These were the gods and goddesses worshiped by the ancient Greeks.

The Olympian gods were human in form. They were not the half beast, half human gods of the Egyptians. They were greater, more powerful and more beautiful than mortal man.

The Greeks prayed to these Olympians for divine help and favors. They offered libations of milk, wine, cake, vegetables or fruit. They also offered sacrifices of bulls, goats, rams or pigs.

There were endless religious festivals in every part of Greece. Athens' great festival the Panathenaea is such an example. There were also shrines and statues to the gods in every part of Greece. The magnificent Parthenon of Athens honored the goddess Athena. At Delphi was the sacred shrine of Apollo.

But the Greeks religion lacked scriptures or dogma. Since they had no strict theology, they were able to question literally everything in the pursuit of truth. And question they did!

Following is a list and description of each of the Olympians:

1. Zeus was the supreme ruler. He was the cloud-gatherer, lord of the sky and the rain god. He also wielded the terrible thunderbolt.

2. Hera was Zeus's wife and sister. She was the protectress of marriage, married women and the home.

3. Poseidon was Zeus's brother and the god of the sea. He also gave the horse to man.

4. Hades was brother to Zeus and Poseidon. He was ruler of the underworld and the dead. (The Greeks, unlike the Egyptians, had a negative concept of the afterlife. Therefore, Hades was not widely worshiped. As Pluto, the god of agriculture, he was very honored.)

5. Pallas Athena was the daughter of Zeus alone. She had no mother. In the *Illiad* she is a battle goddess. Later she is seen as the goddess of reason, wisdom and purity.

6. Apollo was the son of Zeus and Leto. He was the healer, the archer god, sun god, god of light and master musician.

GA1310

7. Artemis was Apollo's twin sister. She was the lady of wild things, the huntress, maiden goddess, and moon goddess.

8. Aphrodite was the goddess of love and beauty. She was "foam-born." In most tales she is the wife of Hephaestus, god of the forge.

9. Hermes was the son of Zeus and messenger to mortals, god of commerce, god of thieves and mischief makers.

10. Ares was the god of war and the son of Zeus and Hera. He was bloodstained and murderous.

11. Hephaestus was the god of fire and artisans. He was ugly and lame and was the protector of smiths.

12. Hestia was the sister of Zeus. She was goddess of the hearth, the symbol of home.

Activities

1. Apply the information presented on the Olympians to identify the Greek gods and goddesses on the following page. Indicate your answers with letters.

_____ 1. Zeus	_____ 7. Artemis
_____ 2. Hera	_____ 8. Aphrodite
_____ 3. Poseidon	_____ 9. Hermes
_____ 4. Hades	_____ 10. Ares
_____ 5. Athena	_____ 11. Hephaestus
_____ 6. Apollo	_____ 12. Hestia

2. Use books on Greek and Roman mythology to find the Roman counterparts for the Greek gods and goddesses. Make a chart like that below.

God or Goddess of	Greek	Roman
Love	Aphrodite	Venus
War		
Sea		
Commerce		

3. After you identify the Greek gods and goddesses on the next page, color each one of them with crayons, colored pencils or pens. Take a piece of white poster board and draw a mountain that covers most of the poster. Cut out the figures of the gods and goddesses and paste them in a group near the top of the mountain. Color the mountain, vegetation, trees and the sky. At the bottom of your poster print *Gods and Goddesses on Mt. Olympus.*

Greek Gods and Goddesses

a

b

c

d

e

f

g

h

i

j

k

l

5

The Greek Statue

There were marvelous statues all over ancient Greece. There were statues of Zeus, Poseidon, Athena, Apollo, Aphrodite, Artemis and other gods and goddesses. There were also beautiful ones of warriors, horsemen, athletes, farmers, young boys, young girls, comic figures, etc.

In this exercise you are going to make a Greek statue of any subject you choose. Look carefully at several books on Greek art and on the Greeks to find the statue you wish to create.

You will need a hammer and two nails, different sizes of strong thin wire, wire cutters, pliers, a small block of wood, modeling clay, toothpicks, a spatula and a small container of water.

First, take the wire and make it into a framework for your statue. Make the body, head, arms and legs. Nail both ends of the leg wires to the wood block. With wire, create a small wire glove on the end of each of the arms.

Next, take modeling clay and start forming the body, head, arms and legs by pressing the clay into and around the wire. Cover the nails with clay and make the form of a foot over each nail. Put clay hands on the wire gloves on the ends of the arms. Dip your fingers in water and smooth out all the parts of your statue.

With a toothpick and spatula, distinguish all features of the statue. Again use water to smooth out the features. Cover the wooden block with clay to complete the statue.

6

GA1310

If you want a decorative band to go around the head or elsewhere, roll out a thin strip of clay. Make decorations on it with a toothpick or spatula once you have placed the strip of clay on the body. For a helmet, press out a round piece of clay for the crown or plume.

When the statue is completed, leave it in its natural color like those of the Greek statues. Then write a complete report on what your statue is and how you made it. Be as detailed as possible.

7

GA1310

Map of the Ancient Greek World

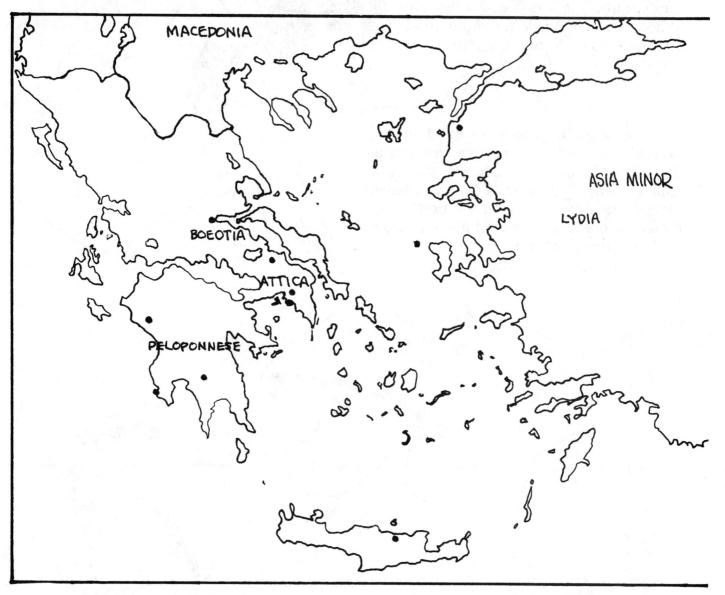

Above is a map of the ancient Greek world. After you have studied several such maps in books on ancient Greece, fill in the correct name by each dot on the map. Several names are already provided on the map for you.

You are to correctly locate Troy, Thermopylae, Delphi, Thebes, Marathon, Athens, Piraeus, Corinth, Olympia, Pylos, Sparta and Cnossus. Also fill in the names of the seas and the Greek islands of Melos, Paros, Naxos, Delos, Tinos and Andros.

If you wish, you may also place additional names on the map.

Illustrate your map in the proper colors. If you wish, also put small drawings such as soldiers, ships, etc., on different parts of the map.

Study this map *several* times in order to draw it from memory. If you are able to do this, you will receive a special grade.

8

Egypt and Tigris-Euphrates

Egypt and the Tigris-Euphrates area were both centers of early civilizations. A map of both areas is drawn for you on this page. You are to label important towns and rivers and then illustrate the map. (Books on ancient civilizations will provide information for you.)

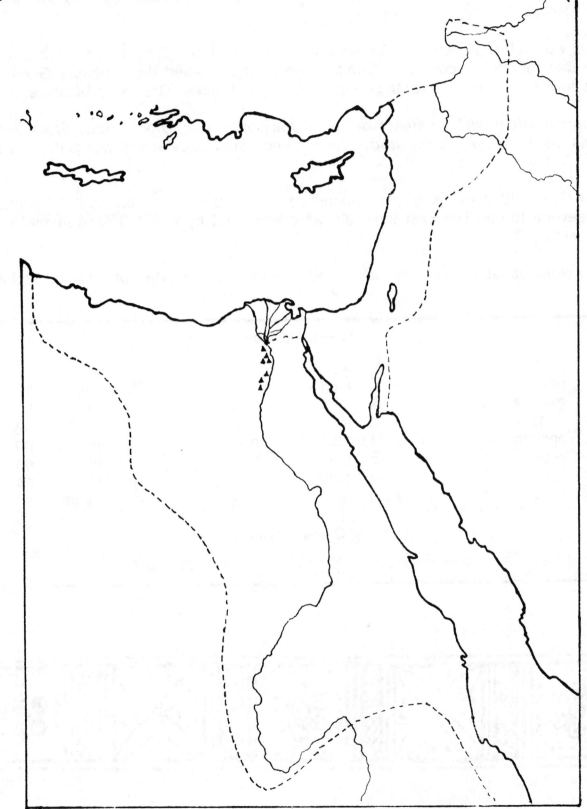

9

GA1310

Greek Words and Alphabet

There are several interesting facts about Greek words. One concerns the words *Greece* and *Greeks*. The people we call Greeks never used these words. In the *Iliad* of Homer these people were called Achaeans. Later they were called Hellenes. The country was called Hellas.

Our words for Greece and Greeks come from the Latin. There was a minor Greek tribe that founded a colony at Cumae. The Romans called these people *Graeci* and were soon using this term for the people and country we call Greeks and Greece.

Approximately twelve percent of our words come from Greek roots. *Stoic, school, drama, barbarian, academy, despot, history* and *chronology* are all words derived from Greek.

The Greek alphabet, taken from Phoenician script about eighth century B.C., eventually had several forms. The East Ionic alphabet was used by all of Greece at the end of fifth century B.C.

The word *alphabet* comes from *alpha* and *beta*, the first two letters of the Greek alphabet.

Greek Alphabet

A	alpha	a	I	iota	i	P	rho	r
B	beta	b	K	kappa	k	Σ	sigma	s
Γ	gamma	g	Λ	lambda	l	T	tau	t
Δ	delta	d	M	mu	m	Υ	upsilon	u,y
E	epsilon	e	N	nu	n	Φ	phi	ph
Z	zeta	z	Ξ	i	x	X	chi	ch
H	eta	e	O	omicron	o	Ψ	psi	ps
Θ	theta	th	Π	pi	p	Ω	omega	o

Greek Words

stoikos—stoic   schole—school

GA1310

Activities

1. In a dictionary such as *Webster's New Collegiate Dictionary*, look up *stoic, school, barbarian* and *academy*. For each word write down the Greek word it came from.

2. Do some browsing on your own and see if you are able to find ten more words derived from the Greek. Write down these words and their meanings past and present.

3. On a separate piece of paper print the entire Greek alphabet as shown in this section. When you finish, illustrate the rest of the page with Greek figures and scenes.

4. The Greek alphabet was taken from Phoenician script. Study the history of the Phoenicians and present a complete report on these people to your teacher and the class.

GREEK WORDS (English Transliteration)	ANCIENT GREEK MEANING	ENGLISH DERIVATIVE
ΠΟΙΗΤΗΣ (poietes)	Creator, poet	Poet
ΠΡΑΚΤΙΚΗ (praktike)	Business, practical knowledge	Practical
ΣΤΩΙΚΟΣ (stoikos)	Stoic, philosopher	Stoic
ΣΧΟΛΗ (schole)	Free time, leisure discussion	School
ΤΥΡΑΝΝΟΣ (tyrannos)	Tyrant, dictator	Tyrant

11

GA1310

Greek Scroll

1. Go to the grocery store and ask someone in the meat department to give you two and a half feet of white or brown wrapping paper. Or you can tape several sheets of white paper together.

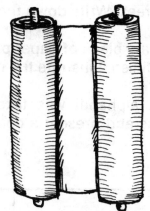

2. Get two dowels or small round pieces of wood (poles). Glue each end of the long strip of paper to a pole. Roll the paper up halfway on each pole.

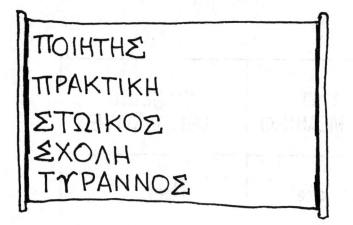

ΠΟΙΗΤΗΣ

ΠΡΑΚΤΙΚΗ

ΣΤΩΙΚΟΣ

ΣΧΟΛΗ

ΤΥΡΑΝΝΟΣ

3. Next unroll your scroll completely. Copy the Greek words that are on the preceding page on the white or brown paper. Use a black felt tip pen or marker.

4. After you copy the words on the scroll and the lettering has dried, leave your scroll unrolled. Take your right hand and gently crinkle up sections of the scroll to give it an ancient effect.

5. When you finish crinkling the paper, roll your scroll up and tie a piece of leather or a piece of colored cloth around it.

GA1310

The City-State

Ancient Greece was composed of endless city-states. The city-state, the *polis*, was a political organization. It meant the city, the land around it and all of the population. It symbolized home, nation, country and religion. Since the city-state was so small, every citizen participated directly in the life and government of the polis.

The Greeks apparently didn't believe in large city-states. Aristotle believed that the city-state should be small enough so that every citizen would know each other. Plato thought the best size for a city-state was 5040 citizens. These citizens meant the males who could vote. The total population of this state would probably have been around 50,000. The population of Athens in its glory was about 300,000, and it was the largest in Greece. Thebes, Sparta, Corinth and other city-states were much smaller.

The Greeks' love and veneration for their city-state made political union of all the city-states impossible. They simply would not band together politically. Each preferred to be a distinct political entity. Athens and Sparta tried to mold all the city-states into an empire, but they failed. Macedonia tried and was briefly successful.

They would, however, come together as a unit when they were all being threatened by a foreign power such as Persia. Athens, Sparta and other Greek city-states turned back and destroyed the Persians.

All the Greek city-states made great contributions to Greek culture. Athens was the greatest, but Sparta, Corinth, Thebes and many other city-states also contributed to the Hellenic civilization.

Activities

1. Study the history of either Thebes or Corinth in order to make an oral class presentation.

2. In planning a city-state, the Greeks first built a fort on a high flat hill (acropolis). Homes and other buildings eventually formed around it. The streets were laid out in rows and crossed at right angles. The houses and other buildings were in a "block" form between the streets. There was a wall around the entire city. On the exercise sheet on the next page, you are to plan an ancient Greek city. The hill for your acropolis and the wall around your city are already drawn. After you study several pictures of ancient Greek cities, plan your own and sketch it on the exercise sheet. And by all means, illustrate it.

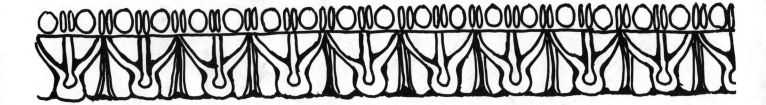

GA1310

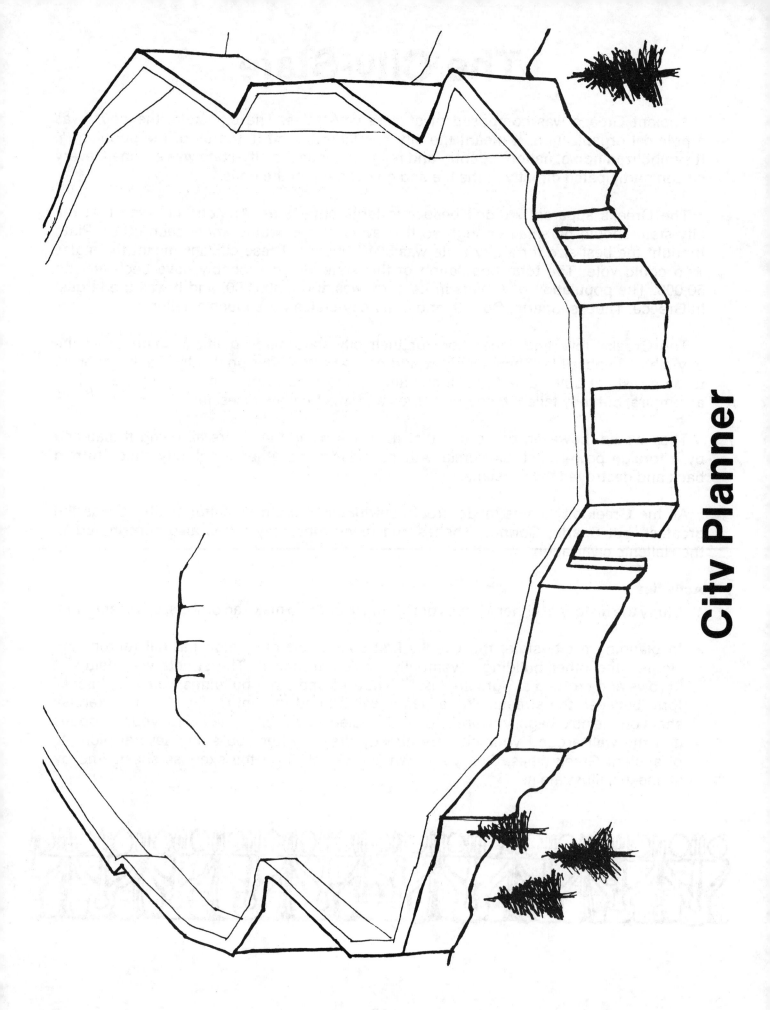

City Planner

14

Athens

Some of the greatest cities in history are Athens of the Golden Age, Rome of the Republic and the Empire, Florence of the Italian Renaissance, London of the Empire, and New York City during modern times.

Of all of these, Athens of the Golden Age is the most famous. The Athens of the Acropolis, the Parthenon and Pericles is world renowned.

Athens sits on a plain close to the southern end of Attica, a peninsula that stretches southeast into the Aegean Sea. All around the city spreads the plain of Attica. Mountains surround the plain except in the southwest. Athens is five miles from Piraeus, Athens' seaport.

Athens was one of the first city-states. (Remember that each state consisted of a city and the land that surrounded it and provided food for the people.)

The city was named for Athena, the goddess of wisdom and the city's patron. About 1900 B.C., Greeks took over Attica and the name *Athens* appears in history. The early population consisted of families and tribes and was governed by kings descended from Erechtheus, an early king of Athens. In the 700's and 600's this kingship was replaced by an oligarchy of magistrates elected by the aristocrats of Athens.

After they had finished their terms of office, the magistrates (archons) became members of the Areopagus, a council of elder statesmen. The Areopagus prepared political matters for the vote of the general assembly and judged murder trials.

As this city-state grew larger, a crisis arose between the small farmers and the aristocrats. Because of this, economic and social reforms were instituted by Solon in 594 B.C. In 508 B.C. Cleisthenes made reforms that made Athens the first democracy.

In the two Persian Wars (490 B.C. and 480-479 B.C.), Athens played a major role in defeating Persia. After this Athens became an empire. The sixty years after the Persian Wars were the most brilliant in the history of Athens. Aristophanes, Aeschylus, Sophocles and other great men helped make Athens the creative center of Greece.

The Peloponnesian War (431-404 B.C.) destroyed the Athenian empire. Athens surrendered to Sparta and she never regained her leadership. But Athens was still the intellectual center of Greece under both Macedonian and Roman rule.

GA1310

Questions

1. What are five of the greatest cities in history? _____ _____
   _____ _____ _____

2. The plain of _____ surrounds Athens.

3. The city was named for _____.

4. The Areopagus is _____

5. 490 B.C. and 480-479 B.C. are the dates of the _____.

6. The _____ destroyed the Athenian empire.

Activity

In order to learn more about some famous Greeks, research one of the following:

Democritus   Thucydides
Xenophon   Herodotus
Demosthenes   Pindar
Callicrates   Hesoid
Sappho

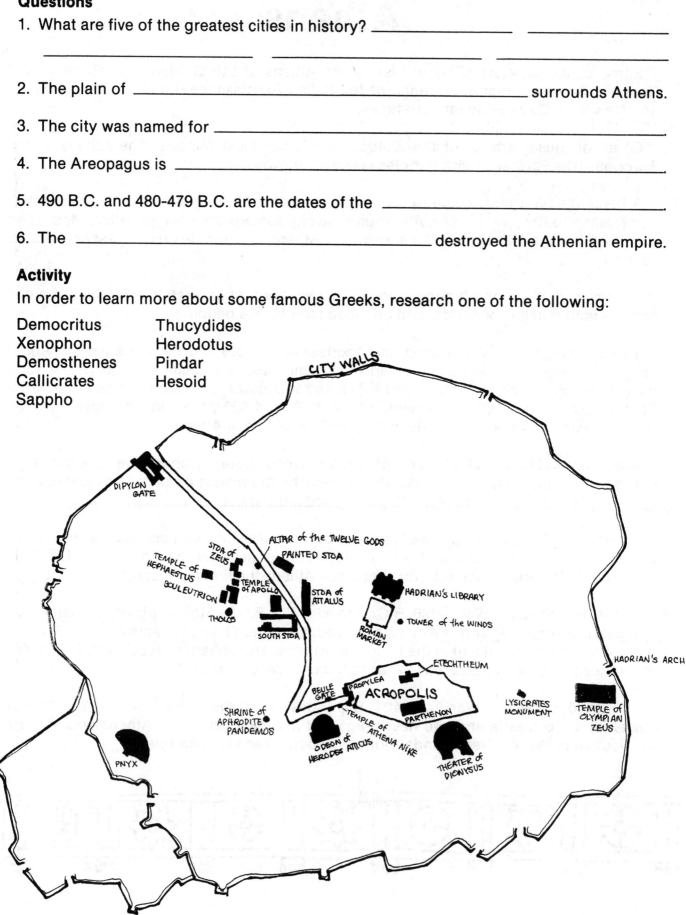

Symbols

A symbol is a word, a drawing, a statue, etc., that has a meaning or several meanings. We recognize symbols. We know what they mean. Below are several symbols. How many do you know?

How many other symbols do you know? Make a chart like this and draw your symbols on it.

17

The Acropolis

The ancient Greeks built Athens around a flat-topped limestone rock called the Acropolis. This was the religious shrine and the fortress of the early Athenians. The word *Acropolis* means "high city." Through the years the Athenians built public buildings and temples on it. Around 1200 B.C. the Athenians built a wall around most of the Acropolis. Around 530 B.C. the Athenians built a temple on the Acropolis and dedicated it to Athena. In 480 B.C. the Persians captured Athens and destroyed most of the buildings on the Acropolis.

Fifth century B.C. was Athens' golden age. In the early part of that century, the Athenians played a leading role in destroying the might of Persia at Marathon and Salamis.

In 447 B.C. the Athenians began to rebuild the Acropolis under the leadership of Pericles. They built many new structures including the magnificent Parthenon, the best known temple in history.

Pericles also started the Propylaea, the huge entrance to the Acropolis. But it was never completed because the Peloponnesian War started in 431 B.C. To the right of the Propylaea stands the small temple of Athena Nike. About sixty yards from the Parthenon is the Erechtheum, a temple dedicated to Athena, Poseidon and Erechtheus, a famous king of early Athens.

The Theater of Dionysus is southeast of the Acropolis. Southwest of the Acropolis is Odeon, a theater. Northwest of the Acropolis was the marketplace of ancient Athens. It was called the Agora. The Stoa of Attalus housed many shops. It stood along the east side of the Agora.

Right outside the Agora stands the Temple of Hephaestus. About 400 yards east of the Theater of Dionysus stood the Temple of Olympian Zeus. This was the largest temple ever built in Greece.

Questions

1. Acropolis means _____

2. The _____ is the best known temple in history.

3. The Athenians began to rebuild the Acropolis under the leadership of _____

4. _____ was a famous king of early Athens.

5. The marketplace of early Athens was called _____

Activities

1. Several thousand years have passed since the buildings and statues on the Acropolis were constructed. What are the most famous buildings and statues of the modern world? Give reasons for your answers.

2. Research the buildings on the Acropolis by using encyclopedias on Classical Greece and books on Greek art and architecture. Choose one building, other than the Parthenon, and present a *complete* description of it. Do a sketch of the building to the best of your ability.

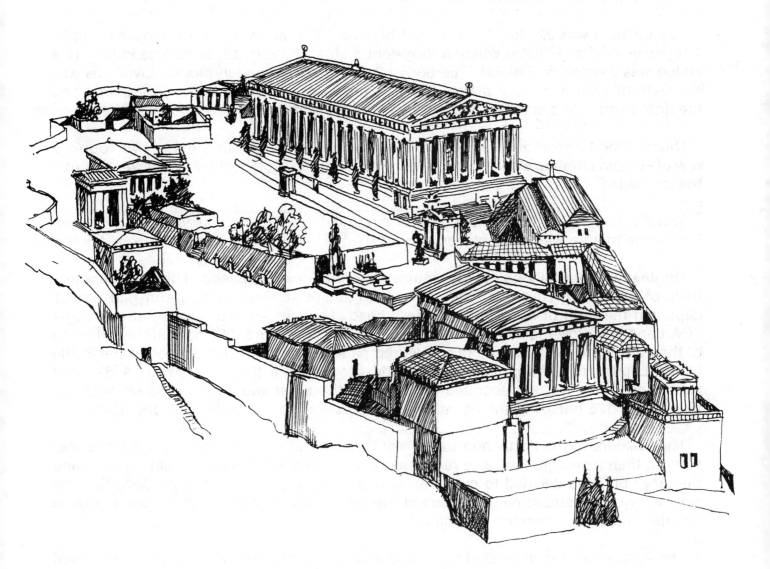

19

The Parthenon

In 449 B.C. the great Athenian statesman Pericles asked the sculptor Phidias to rebuild the Acropolis. Phidias decided to begin a shrine to Athena. This was the magnificent Parthenon, "dwelling of the maiden." The older Parthenon had been raised in 488 to celebrate Athens' victory at Marathon. Eight years later the invading Persians burned it down while it was still half built.

It took two years of planning before the new Parthenon was begun. The first stone was laid on July 28, 447 B.C. Phidias hired the leading architects and sculptors to build it. The temple was designed by Callicrates, Mnesicles and Ictinus.

The building was 228 feet long, 65 feet high and 101 feet wide. Its design was simple. There was one large room where a forty-foot statue of the goddess Athena stood. This statue was created by Phidias. The body was of shaped wooden blocks. Over this was a sheath of gold and ivory plates. Its left hand rested upon a twenty-foot shield and the right hand held a statue of Nike, the goddess of victory.

Next to the large room was the temple treasury room. Around these two rooms a row of columns formed a colonnade. There were forty-six Doric columns that went around the four sides.

The Parthenon was built throughout of the finest marble that was very light in color. This white marble was brought from Mount Pentelicus, eleven miles away from Athens.

Originally, beautifully painted sculpture decorated the Parthenon. The two triangular ends of the roof (pediments) were filled with sculpture. The eastern end had scenes depicting the birth of Athena from Zeus's head. The western end showed the struggle of Athena and Poseidon for possession of Attica. Above the columns, around the top of the outer wall, were a series of sculptured panels depicting such scenes as the Battle of the Lapiths and the centaurs and battle scenes from the Trojan War. A 524-foot continuous Ionic frieze (decorated band) along the outer wall of the cella showed 350 people and 125 horses in the Panathenaic procession honoring the birthday of Athena.

The builders of the Parthenon had a real problem. In architecture nothing looks less straight than a straight line. The rectilinear floor plan created the problem. Phidias and the other builders decided to create an optical illusion. They did this by distorting the symmetry of the structure. They canted the pillars and bowed the sides out to create a perfect vision of geometric perfection.

The Parthenon was dedicated to Athena and clearly showed that the gods controlled the world. But, in reality, the Parthenon was a symbol. It clearly stated the might and glory of Athens and the Athenian people. It glorified the Persian host. It stated, "Here is Athens, the glory of the world."

GA1310

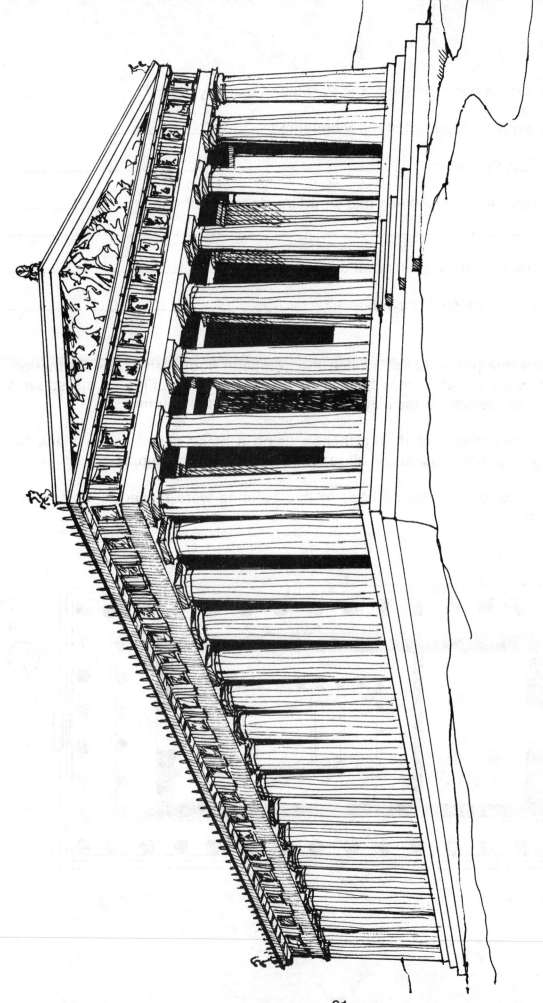

Restoration of the Parthenon, Northwest

21

Questions

1. On what date did the construction of the Parthenon actually begin? _____

2. What great sculptor had control of the rebuilding? _____

3. How long was the Parthenon? _____

4. Describe the great statue of Athena that stood inside the Parthenon. _____

   _____

5. What type of column was used in rebuilding the Parthenon? _____

6. What did the Parthenon clearly symbolize? _____

Activities

1. On a piece of white poster board, sketch the complete floor plan of the Parthenon. Next, go over your sketch with a black felt tip pen for the outline of the squares and a black magic marker for the black circles that depict the columns.

2. Make a complete drawing of the Parthenon using a black pencil and a black felt tip pen. Carefully shade and blacken all required sections of the temple.

3. Research how the tons of marble used in this building were moved to its site and write a report on it.

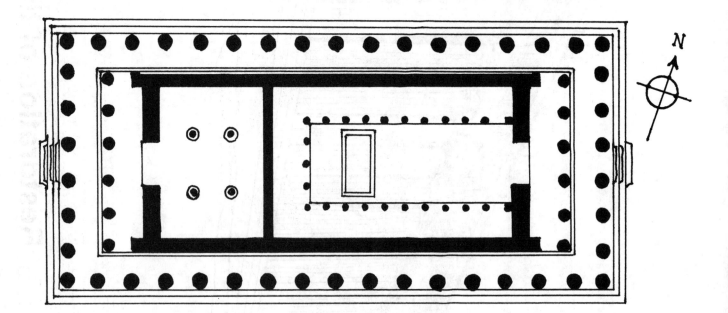

GA1310

Statue of Athena

Greek Columns

On this page are three columns. The next page shows the capitals and the bases for Doric, Ionic and Corinthian columns. You are to cut these out and correctly paste each pair on a column on this page. Draw in the proper design for each column. A book on Greek architecture will guide you.

GA1310

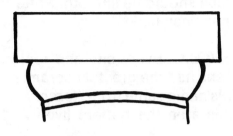

DORIC CAPITAL

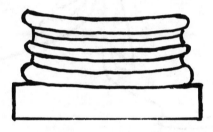

PLATFORM
DORIC COLUMN RESTS ON

IONIC CAPITAL

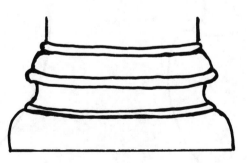

IONIC BASE
and PLINTH

CORINTHIAN CAPITAL

CORINTHIAN BASE

Greek Pottery

Pottery is one of man's oldest art forms. The pottery maker has only his hands and a few tools to use. But clay lends itself to shaping. The shape of each product must be considered and since pottery must be handled, the surface should be smooth. Pottery calls for decoration and every type of design conceivable has been used.

In Greece the potter's art probably began as early as 550 B.C. Every city and region there had its own type of pottery. In sixth century B.C., Athens had the greatest ceramists in all of Greece. The Greek word for ceramics is *keramos*. This name came from *Keramikos*, a part of Athens near or around the Dipylon Gate. In this area the potters lived and produced their wares.

The Greeks produced endless types of pottery. Most of them have been equaled. They made bowls, vases, drinking cups, etc. Their surfaces were decorated with endless different scenes that depicted various aspects of Greek life.

Here are some basic types of Greek pottery.

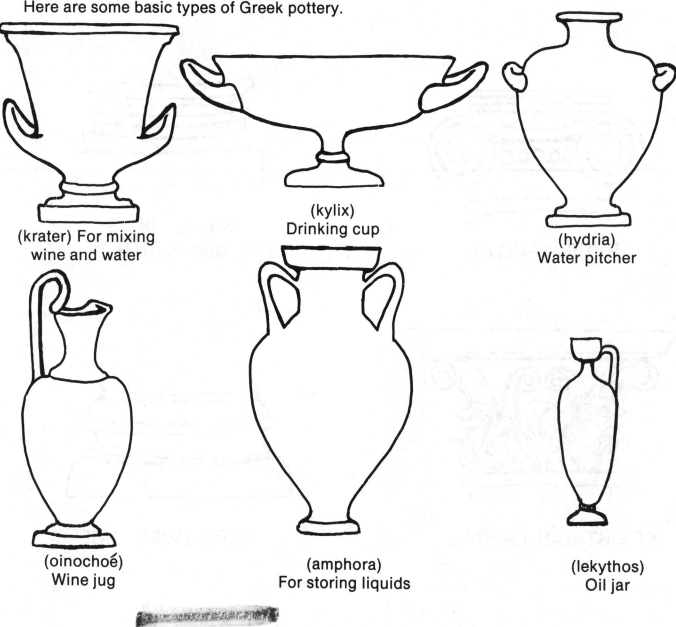

(krater) For mixing wine and water

(kylix) Drinking cup

(hydria) Water pitcher

(oinochoé) Wine jug

(amphora) For storing liquids

(lekythos) Oil jar

GA1310

Greek Pottery Styles

The Greek potters decorated their pottery in two styles. The black-figure style was a method where the design was painted in black over the red natural color of the clay.

You can duplicate this method by using a black felt tip pen and making your sketches on red construction paper.

Sketch your designs with the black felt tip pen. Cover the inside of each design in black but leave red lines showing to distinguish your designs.

Using a black felt tip pen, sketch Greek vase or jar designs on a piece of red construction paper. Follow the other instructions to complete your designs. Hand your paper in to your teacher.

The red-figure method of decorating pottery possibly began in fifth century B.C. The figures and scenes were left in the natural red of the clay. The background was covered with solid black.

For the red-figure method, sketch your designs on red construction paper. Go over your designs with a black felt tip pen, but do not fill in the designs with black. Leave them in red. Paint the background completely with black paint.

GA1310

Sketch your new designs on red construction paper. Go over your designs with a black felt tip pen. Finish your designs by following the rest of the directions. Put a border around the four sides of the paper. Turn your drawing in to the teacher.

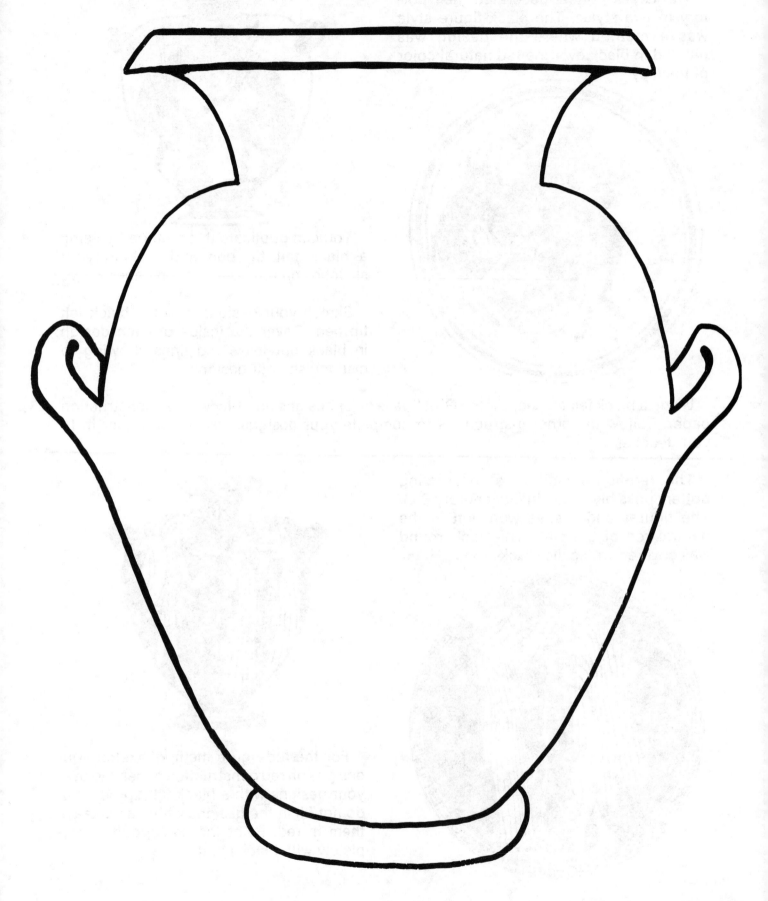

28

Greek Pottery Identification

On this sheet are six types of Greek pottery you have just read about and seen. Under each one you are to print the correct Greek name and information about its use. After you have done this, you are to decorate each type with various Greek scenes. Use the black-figure method on the top three and red-figure method on the bottom three. Books on Greece and Greek art will provide you with examples of such scenes.

GA1310

Sparta

Sparta was the second best known city-state in Greece. But she and Athens were at opposite ends of the pole. Athens was democratic and artistic. Sparta was a military state and a closed society.

Sparta lay in one of the southernmost valleys of the Peloponnesus. Its land was fertile and well-watered. The city was surrounded on three sides by mountains—an excellent defense.

There were three classes of people in the Spartan state. There were the Spartans, descendants of the Dorians who conquered most of the Greek peninsula around 1000 B.C. They were the ruling class. Next, were the Helots who were slaves of the state. They did most of the work. Finally, there was a class of free farmers and craftsmen who performed many tasks and labored in the fields, but like the Helots they had no vote in the government. Only the aristocratic Spartans controlled the government.

All of this free time allowed the Spartans to do what they did for centuries—become the best soldiers in the world. All citizens, male and female, were rigorously trained from birth in all physical aspects. All boys were taken from their families at the age of seven and went to live in barracks. Thus began their only career—that of a soldier.

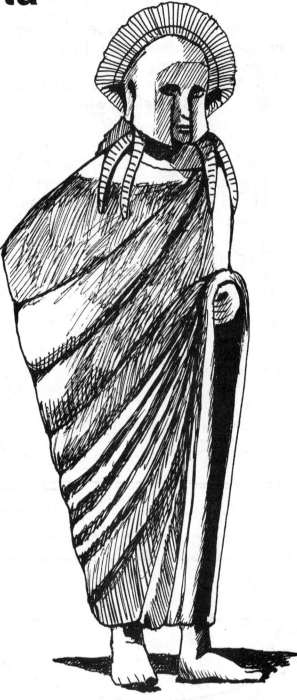

SPARTAN SOLDIER

They lived in barracks, ate from a common mess and slept on rush palliasses. They learned total obedience, superhuman endurance and the skills of a soldier. Their heads were close-shaved, and they marched barefoot on many occasions.

GA1310

They were never to flinch from punishment or show any expression of pain or fear. The famous story of the Spartan boy who hid a fox he had stolen under his tunic and allowed the fox to gnaw through his belly rather than admit the. theft is an example of such training and obedience.

At the age of twenty and until he was thirty, the young Spartan was a cadet who guarded the borders of Sparta, policed the country and kept the slaves in order. Once a year the Spartans declared an official war on the Helots and killed any they thought to be rebellious or who showed potential leadership.

When he was thirty, the Spartan was considered mature and enjoyed the duties and rights of citizenship. He usually married at this time. When he was sixty, his career in the military was over and he either trained the young or engaged in public service.

The Spartan soldier was terrifying in combat. Wearing garlands on their heads and marching to the piper's religious hymn, they marched in total order towards the enemy. Once engaged, they fought with great skill and showed neither fury nor fear. It has been stated that Sparta lost only two battles in five hundred years.

Unlike young Athenian girls, who lived the most secluded lives, Spartan women were the freest in Greece. On the same footing as the men, they participated in many sports in public. They learned to throw the discus, they wrestled and they learned the use of the javelin, an instrument of war. All of this produced healthy young women who eventually became healthy mothers who produced children for the state.

Sparta conquered Athens during the Peloponnesian War in 404 B.C. But the Greek states revolted against Spartan cruelty and defeated her in 371 B.C.

Unlike Athens, Sparta produced no great men and no great works of art or architecture. All an archaeologist can find of her today is rubble and stone.

Questions

1. How many classes of people were there in Sparta? _____

2. Describe each class. _____

_____

3. Boys were taken from their families at age _____.

4. At what age did the Spartan soldier marry? _____

_____

5. How were Spartan girls different from other Greek girls?

_____

6. How many battles did Sparta lose in five hundred years?

_____

Activities

1. Young Nazi boys and girls were trained in somewhat the same manner as the youth of Sparta. In books such as *The Rise and Fall of the Third Reich*, you find information concerning this training. After you have read about this training, consider these questions: "Should a state or nation have such a universal training plan as this? What type of training, if any, should it be? Is this type of training dangerous to the individual being trained and to outsiders?" (This subject would make a strong class discussion.)

2. In books on Greek armor and warfare, learn all you can about the weapons, armor and battle tactics of the Spartan soldier for a written and illustrated report.

GA1310

The Persian Wars

Darius, King of Persia, controlled Asia Minor. This included the Greek cities in Ionia. In 499 B.C. these cities rebelled against the Persians, and other Greeks came to their aid. Athens was one that helped. In 490 B.C., Darius decided to teach the upstart Athenians a lesson.

Marathon—An army of Medes and Persians, 20,000 men, landed at the bay of Marathon, twenty-five miles northwest of Athens. The Greeks met them with a force of 10,000 Athenians and 1000 Plateans.

Before the battle, the Athenians sent Pheidippides, the fastest runner in Greece, to bring help from Sparta which was 150 miles away. But the Spartans wouldn't come because of a religious festival and didn't get there until after the battle. Supposedly, Pheidippides ran through the hills between Athens and Sparta in two days.

33

GA1310

The Greeks had been watching the Persians from the hills around Marathon. The Athenian general Miltiades decided to take the Persians by surprise. He knew he was outnumbered and ordered an attack on the run. Herodotus stated that this was the first time in history that Greeks ran towards an enemy. The Persians must have thought the Greeks were crazy.

But this lightning attack won the day for the Athenians. They drove the Persians back to their ships. The Persians suffered heavy losses. Herodotus said the Athenians lost 192 men and the Persians 6400.

At the shoreline, the Athenians overpowered seven Persian ships, but the rest of the fleet sailed away. Miltiades was afraid the Persian fleet would attack Athens and that the city, not knowing of the victory at Marathon, might surrender so he sent Pheidippides, already exhausted from running to Sparta and back, to tell the Athenians of the victory. Pheidippides raced the twenty-five miles to Athens, feebly uttered the words "Rejoice, we conquer" and died.

Miltiades and the Athenians, marching at top speed, got to Athens before the Persians. The Persian fleet lay at anchor outside the harbor of the city and eventually sailed away.

GA1310

Thermopylae—Xerxes became king of Persia after his father's death in 486 B.C. He decided to invade Greece to avenge the defeat at Marathon. Gathering a huge army (Herodotus said it was 2.5 million men, but it was probably nearer 300,000), he invaded Greece from the northeast in 480 B.C. This army was also supported by 800 triremes (warships). Athens and the other city-states banded together to face this vast host.

The Greeks met them at the narrow pass at Thermopylae. It was a perfect place for a small army to hold off a larger one. Here King Leonidas of Sparta with 300 Spartans and a few thousand other Greeks fought against odds of nearly forty to one. They, especially the Spartans, were magnificent. Neither hails of arrows nor the charge of Xerxes' immortals could break them. For two days they held the pass.

Greek traitors led the Persians through little known mountain passes, and they surrounded Leonidas and the other Greeks. Leonidas sent most of the other Greeks away. He and the Spartans fought to the death. Only one Spartan got home alive and no one spoke to him the rest of his life. The fierce onslaught of the Spartans destroyed many noble Persians. Two of Xerxes' brothers were killed. A simple stone monument was placed there after the war was over. The inscription reads: "Go tell the Spartans, stranger passing by, that here obedient to their will we lie."

GA1310

Salamis—After Thermopylae was lost, the Persians poured through the pass and moved toward Athens. The Athenians asked the oracle at Delphi what they should do and the oracle said they would be saved by wooden walls.

A little after the Battle of Marathon, the Athenians had discovered silver mines and the city became wealthy. There was a proposal that every citizen should share the wealth, but Themistocles persuaded them to put the money into warships. At the beginning of this new Persian attack, they had a fleet of 200 such ships. These ships, Themistocles told them, were the wooden walls that would save them.

Athens was to be abandoned. All its people fled to other parts of Greece or to the island of Salamis. The Greek army and fleet went to Salamis and awaited the Persians. Themistocles sent a false message to the Persians telling them the Greek fleet was planning to escape in the night. The Persians were lured into the narrower waters of the Salamis channel. Here the Greeks, on September 23, 480 B.C., destroyed them. What was left of the Persian fleet sailed for home.

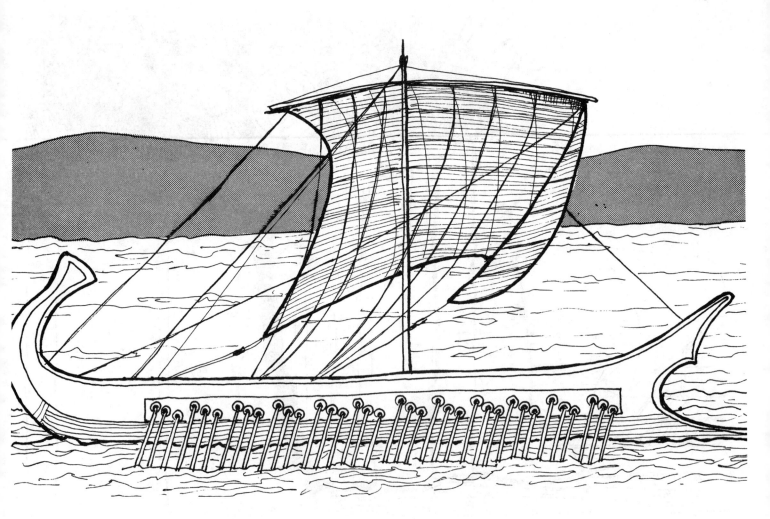

Platae—Xerxes saw his fleet scattered and destroyed, and he decided to gather his army and go back to Asia. He left behind half of his army in northern Greece. The next spring this half of Xerxes' army moved south. They were met by around 100,000 Greeks from almost all the city-states. The Persians were crushed. The great victory mainly belonged to the magnificent Spartan soldiers. Xerxes' power was broken. Greece was left to do as she would.

Questions

1. The Athenian general at Marathon was _____.

2. Who was Pheidippides? _____

3. Why did the Persians attack Athens? _____

4. _____ was the war leader of the Spartans at Thermopylae.

5. _____ destroyed the Persian fleet at Salamis.

6. What soldiers were responsible for the Persians defeat at Platae? _____

GA1310

The Marathon

The Marathon was not one of the events in the ancient Olympic Games. For a long time over the centuries, the Greeks had tried to think of a way to honor Pheidippides' great run. In the first international Olympic Games in Athens in 1896, they decided they would hold a "Marathon" race. They would re-create his twenty-five-mile run from Marathon to Athens.

On April 10, 1896, twenty-five young men started running toward Athens. In Athens' Panathenaic Stadium around 70,000 spectators awaited them. Thousands of Greeks stood along the road from Marathon to Athens watching the race and encouraging the runners.

A young Greek shepherd named Spiridon Loues won the Marathon and the Marathon run became an important part of the Olympic Games.

The original twenty-five miles of the first Marathon run was changed to a distance of 26 miles, 385 yards in 1908. The famous Boston Marathon is 26.2 miles from the start at Hopkinton to the finish at Pru.

The marathon is a very long and demanding race. It is twice as long as most distance races and is very long in terms of time. It is also physically and psychologically demanding.

After you and some friends or the entire class have spent some time researching books on running, running events and the Boston Marathon, you are to plan out a marathon course that runs through your town. You will have to measure the 26 miles, 385 yards from point to point.

In the box below draw and label every part of your marathon. Any needed explanation(s) should be neatly printed.

MARATHON

START

FINISH

GA1310

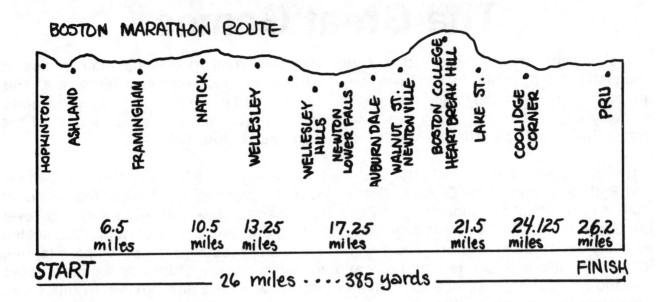

BOSTON MARATHON ROUTE

HOPKINTON
ASHLAND
FRAMINGHAM — 6.5 miles
NATICK — 10.5 miles
WELLESLEY — 13.25 miles
WELLESLEY HILLS
NEWTON LOWER FALLS — 17.25 miles
AUBURNDALE
WALNUT ST. NEWTONVILLE
BOSTON COLLEGE HEART BREAK HILL — 21.5 miles
LAKE ST. — 24.125 miles
COOLIDGE CORNER
PRU — 26.2 miles

START _____ 26 miles · · · · 385 yards _____ FINISH

In the initial stages of your planning, it would be a good idea for all of you to walk the entire length of your marathon so you will have a good idea of how long such a run is.

Remember, you will have to know the exact distance of each point along your route.

When you have completed your route, find out if there are any marathon runners in your area and ask them if they would like to run your marathon.

The Great Games

The ancient Greeks thought that it was very important to develop their bodies as completely as possible. In their religious festivals, athletics played a large role. This athletic competition, they believed, honored the spirits of the dead and pleased the gods. In every city in Greece young men and boys exercised and prepared for one of the great athletic festivals. These festivals may have begun before 1400 B.C.

Eventually, four national festivals developed. These were the Isthmian, Nemean, Olympic and Pythian Games. The Olympic Games were the greatest. Held every four years at Athens in honor of the supreme god Zeus, these games drew competitors from all over the Greek world. The contests took place in the great Stadium of Olympia that seated as many as 40,000 spectators. There were foot races, wrestling, the *pentathlon* (sprint, long jump, discus throw, javelin throw and wrestling), boxing, four-horse chariot races and the *pancration*, a savage sport that combined wrestling and boxing. In this sport, which was introduced in 648 B.C., some competitors were killed.

The winners of the Olympic Games, crowned with olive wreaths, became heroes of all of Greece and many times of the known world.

Winners of the other games were also presented garlands—parsley at the Nemean Games, laurel at the Pythian Games and pine needles at the Isthmian Games.

Sometimes winners at the Games received a great deal of money or many vases of olive oil.

40

GA1310

Activities

1. The Pythian Games were second in importance to the Olympic Games. They were held every four years in honor of the god Apollo. In an encyclopedia, find information on these games and prepare a complete written report on them for your teacher.

2. Make a list of all the events in the Summer Games of the modern Olympics.

3. For extra credit, do the same for the Winter Games.

GA1310

Homer

The two greatest epics in Western literature, the *Iliad* and the *Odyssey*, were authored by the blind poet Homer. He was probably a bard who lived in Asia Minor or on one of the islands near there. Some state he was born on the island of Chios in the Aegean Sea before the year 800 B.C.

When he started putting the *Iliad* and the *Odyssey* together, he had a great deal of ancient material to work with. And it was ancient! The Trojan War of the *Iliad* probably took place around 1250 B.C.

The material Homer worked with was lays that described the Mycenaeans of the Greek Heroic Age (1500-1150 B.C.). These people were a warrior society that was in almost constant warfare. They raided and plundered other people. Each of their towns had a highly fortified citadel of huge stone blocks. Around 1200 B.C. a wave of invaders, the Dorians, began attacking the Mycenaeans, and in a hundred years all their strongholds had fallen.

Many of the Mycenaeans fled to Asia Minor. Homer was possibly descended from a family that went to Ionia after the Dorian conquest.

After Homer had composed the two epics, "stitcher of songs," the rhapsodists began to recite the new compositions just as they had the earlier lays. Thus the epics were spread over all the Greek world.

The first written forms of these epics may have occurred around 650 B.C.

Activities

1. Write a full report on Homer and turn it in to your teacher.

2. The *Iliad* and the *Odyssey* are considered the world's two greatest epics, but there are other epics. Talk to your school librarian and ask her to help you find their names and what country or people they represent.

GA1310

The Trojan War

The *Iliad*, which means "poem about Troy," is an epic. An epic is a long narrative poem written in a dignified style that tells a tale of a great hero or tales of several great heroes.

This epic tells how several bands of the Mycenaeans of the Heroic Age attacked the great city of Troy on the coast of Asia Minor. In the *Iliad*, Homer calls these people Argives, Danaans or Achaeans. These Argives were led by the great Agamemnon, King of Mycenae. With him were his brother Menelaus, King of Sparta, the terrifying Achilles, Diomedes, Odysseus, Nestor, Ajax and many more Greek kings and heroes. The date the war began was 1250 B.C. Historians at one time considered this date to have been 1184 B.C.

The war started supposedly because Paris, a prince of Troy, chose Aphrodite as the "fairest" goddess over Hera, wife of Zeus and Athena, the goddess of wisdom. Each goddess had promised Paris a great reward if he chose her. Aphrodite had promised him the most beautiful woman in the world.

This woman was Helen, the wife of Menelaus, King of Sparta. The goddess caused Helen to fall madly in love with Paris, and they ran off to Troy together.

Menelaus called upon his brother Agamemnon for help. Agamemnon gathered the Argive kings and their warriors together, and this great host sailed to Troy which they lay siege to for ten years before they finally destroyed it.

Set against the Argives' greatest hero, Achilles, is the great Trojan hero, Hector. Both are great warriors, but Hector was fated to die by the gods and Achilles kills him.

The gods and goddesses all participate in the war. Hera and Athena despise Troy and do everything they can to destroy it. Ares, the god of war, and Aphrodite help the Trojans. Other Greek deities all helped one side or the other.

The *Iliad* only covers a few weeks of fighting in the tenth year of the war. But it covers scenes of endless combat, of great heroes fighting and many dying. The *Iliad* glorified war. In battle the true hero emerges. Homer has scene after scene of warriors being killed or dying.

The *Iliad* and its brother epic the *Odyssey* were poems that became all important to the Greeks. These two epics made Homer the best loved, most honored and most respected poet in the history of Greece and perhaps in the history of the world.

43

44

GA1310

One of the great pioneers of archaeology, the German Heinrich Schliemann, discovered the site of Troy in the 1870's.

He was born in 1822 in Neubukow, Mecklenburg, Germany. His father was a poor pastor. As a small boy he fell in love with the *Iliad* and vowed he would one day find the city of Troy. In order to do this, he knew he would have to become wealthy. He was an intelligent lad and he worked hard. By the age of thirty-six, he had become a millionaire.

He now had the funds necessary to search for the legendary city. Many historians during Schliemann's time thought the tales of Homer to be pure legend, but Schliemann found Troy exactly where Homer said it was. The site of the ancient city of Troy was Hissarlik, Turkey. He found not one city but nine, all built on the ruins of the one before. One of these was the Troy of the *Iliad*. In his excavations he also found great treasures.

In 1876-1878 Schliemann uncovered the tombs of the kings of Mycenae on the Greek mainland. He found great riches in their graves. In one he found a gold mask, and he thought he had found the grave of Agamemnon, the leader of the Greek host against the city of Troy, but he was mistaken. The graves were found to be much older.

Questions

1. What goddess did Paris name "fairest"? _____

2. Who was the war leader of the Argives? _____

3. Helen was the wife of _____.

4. An epic is _____.

5. The great Trojan hero is _____.

6. How long did the Argives lay siege to Troy? _____

Activities

1. In a translation of the *Iliad* by W.H.D. Rouse or in "Homer," *Great Books of the Western World*, read Book II about the incident between Thersites and Odysseus. Then write a complete description of Thersites. Also draw a picture of what you think he looks like.

2. If you have the time and interest and are a strong reader, read all of the *Iliad*. Discuss this activity with your teacher to find out how he/she wants you to do it and what he/she expects you to gain from it.

3. In Book I of the *Iliad*, find the names of the major war leaders of the Greeks. List them carefully.

4. Athena, Hera, Apollo and Ares are important goddesses and gods in the *Iliad*. Using encyclopedias, write a full report on any two of them.

GA1310

Great Archaeologists

Archaeologists study the material remains of past human life and activities. They search for, discover and study artifacts, fossil relics and monuments. Some archaeologists have made important discoveries. On this sheet are listed the names of important discoveries. After the name of each discovery, you are to write the name of the archaeologist who made the discovery, the date or dates this took place, where the discovery was made, what was found and the importance of the discovery. (Ask your teacher and librarian for help on this exercise.)

1. Troy _____
_____
_____
_____
_____
_____

2. Tomb of Tutenkhamon _____
_____
_____
_____
_____
_____

3. Machu Picchu _____
_____
_____
_____
_____
_____

4. Palace of Minos at Knossos _____
_____
_____
_____
_____

GA1310

Amateur Archaeologist

You are the leader of a team of archaeologists who have entered a great beehive-formed tomb of a warrior-king of Mycenae. In the center of the tomb you find the treasures pictured on this page. Study them carefully and answer these questions.

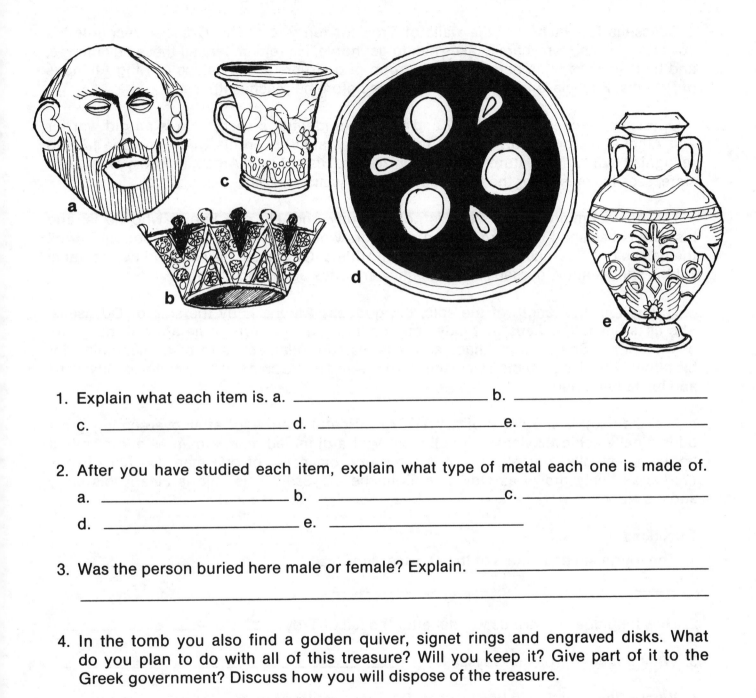

1. Explain what each item is. a. _____ b. _____
   c. _____ d. _____ e. _____

2. After you have studied each item, explain what type of metal each one is made of.
   a. _____ b. _____ c. _____
   d. _____ e. _____

3. Was the person buried here male or female? Explain. _____
   _____

4. In the tomb you also find a golden quiver, signet rings and engraved disks. What do you plan to do with all of this treasure? Will you keep it? Give part of it to the Greek government? Discuss how you will dispose of the treasure.

   _____
   _____
   _____

GA1310

The Wanderings of Odysseus

The *Odyssey* tells the story of the adventurous wanderings of Odysseus as he valiantly attempts to reach Ithaca, his home, to be reunited with his faithful wife Penelope and his beloved son Telemachus.

Odysseus fought before the walls of Troy for ten years. The *Odyssey* recounts his adventures in the ten years it takes him to get home. He remembers all these adventures, and he discusses them before a large group of courtiers at the palace of King Alcinous of Phaecia. Phaecia is the last place he stops before he reaches Ithaca.

Odysseus reaches Ithaca safely and keeps his identity a secret. He is an old warrior and Athena, his protector, has altered his appearance. Even his wife Penelope fails to recognize him. One creature does recognize him. His old dog, Argos, in a very weakened state, sees his master for the first time in twenty years and dies.

The homecoming of Odysseus is not a happy one. No one knows who he is, and his wife is besieged by a large group of suitors who are draining all the food and drink the palace of Odysseus has. With the aid of Athena, Odysseus, his son, and two servants kill the suitors and Odysseus and his family are once again together.

Throughout the length of the epic, the goddess Athena is by the side of Odysseus. She asks her father Zeus that Odysseus be allowed to return home after all his years of wandering. She goes to Ithaca and tells his son Telemachus to begin searching for his father. She also protects Telemachus. At the end of the epic she fully restores Odysseus and his father, Laertes.

The *Odyssey* is the story of a brave resourceful man who, after overcoming great odds, finally achieves victory. It is the story of a dignified man, a man who knows that he will eventually triumph. And it is the story, basically, of one man. No hero in the *Iliad* is as finely drawn as Odysseus is in the *Odyssey*. This epic is clearly his story and his alone.

Questions

1. The four main characters of the *Odyssey* are _____, _____, _____ and _____.

2. How long does Odysseus wander after the fall of Troy? _____

3. What goddess protects Odysseus? _____

4. What is the situation in Ithaca when Odysseus returns home? _____

_____

5. The son of Odysseus is _____

GA1310

Activities

1. Read the last two pages of Book XIII in the *Odyssey* to find out how Athena disguises Odysseus as an old man. Talk to your teacher about this description.

2. Book XXI is the story of the contest with the great bow. Read the story. Close the epic. Then attempt to write down the story from memory.

3. Read the entire *Odyssey* if you have your teacher's permission and if you wish to do so. Keep notes on each book as you read so you will have a strong understanding of this great story of adventure.

ODYSSEUS and DIOMED AMBUSH DOLON, a TROJAN

The Theater

In 534 B.C. in Athens the theater came into being. As part of the celebration of the Great Dionysia (for the god of wine, Dionysus), an annual contest for tragedy was established.

The theater was very important to the Athenians. It was a religious event and one attended by both men and women. The fee to attend was two obols. Anyone too poor to pay this sum was allowed in free. The people sat in seats in the theater of Dionysus, located along the southeast slope of the Acropolis. 14,000 people could attend at one time.

The rules of the contest stated that three dramatists were each to submit four plays—three tragedies and a satyr play (a type of burlesque). Each play was about one and a half hours. The plays were about heroes, myths and legends so the audience knew what they were about. But the audience was more interested in how the playwright handled the material—how he told the story and how it was acted out. Judges had special seats near the performances, and at the end of the contest a winner was chosen among the playwrights. The winning playwright received a prize as well as the fame of winning the contest. Much later, there were prizes for the actors as well as for the plays.

The actors were all men. Women were not allowed to act. The actors wore large masks that amplified their voices. From top to bottom, they were clothed in rich garments. They also wore elevated boots. These accessories made them larger than life, which was the main idea.

Playing both male and female roles, the actors performed the story of the play on the raised stage. The chorus was at ground level. These people danced and sang in unison and made comments on different events that happened during the play.

The three greatest tragic dramatists were Aeschylus, Sophocles and Euripides. The greatest playwright of the comic genre was Aristophanes.

Drama began in Athens and from there it fanned out all over the Greek-speaking world. Eventually, most of the important cities had their own theaters.

Questions

1. When did the theater come into being? _____

2. How much did it cost to attend the theater in Athens?

   _____

3. What were the rules of the contest? _____

   _____

4. What were the plays about? _____

   _____

5. How were the actors dressed? _____

   _____

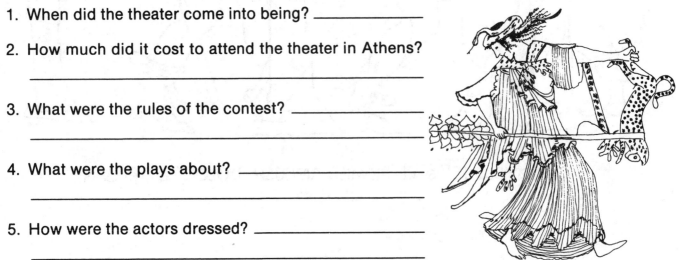

GA1310

51

Activities

1. In an encyclopedia that discusses the theater, look up the Lenaea that was held in January in Athens. Which received the most emphasis at this festival? Was it tragedy or comedy?

2. With your teacher's permission and guidance, read Sophocles' *Antigone*. When you finish, write a short paper stating who you think is right. Was Antigone correct in her actions or was Creon? Your paper should represent your reasons for whichever choice you make.

3. Gather information on the comic genius Aristophanes and list the names of his plays that survive.

4. Who wrote the *Agamemnon* and what is it about? This information can be obtained from an encyclopedia.

5. The word *theatron* meant "seating area." Find the meaning of *orchestra*, *thymele* and *skene*. (Information on the early Greek theater will provide the answers.)

Greek Heroes

Greek dramatists had a vast storehouse of myths, legends and exploits of heroes to draw from in writing their plays. The heroes of Troy were used in plays. *Agamemnon* is a play by Aeschylus that depicts what happens to the conqueror of Troy when he returned home. The legend of Oedipus of Thebes is portrayed by Sophocles in *Oedipus Rex*.

But there were many more heroes. All of them were special mortals. Some were children of the gods. They performed great deeds and have become immortalized in Greek myths and legends. Following is a representation of some of the most famous.

Theseus was one of the greatest heroes of Greek mythology. His father was Aegeus, the king of Athens, and his mother was a Troezen princess. Before Theseus was born, his father left his mother Aethra in Troezen and journeyed back to Athens. Aegeus left his sword and sandals under a great rock. He told his wife that when his son was old enough, he should lift the rock and get the sword and sandals. Then he was to come to Aegeus in Athens.

Theseus eventually lifted the rock and set out for Athens. He had many adventures in his life. He killed bandits and monsters, went to Crete and killed the half human, half bull Minotaur and succeeded in escaping with the aid of Adriadne.

After he became the king of Athens, he led the fight against Thebes, married a beautiful Amazon princess and was a member of the Argonauts as they searched for the Golden Fleece.

GA1310

Heracles (Hercules). In ancient times Heracles was the most widely known of all Greek heroes. He was the son of Zeus and Princess Alcmene, a mortal. After his death, his body was consumed by fire, and he was taken to Olympus where he became a god.

Heracles was given twelve labors to perform to atone for a crime. (1) He killed the lion of Nemea, (2) slew the deadly Hydra of Lerna, (3) captured the Erymantian boar, (4) captured the golden-horned Arcadian stag, (5) drove a flock of ferocious birds away, (6) cleaned the stables of King Augeas by diverting two rivers to flush them out, (7) captured the bull of King Minos, (8) brought the horses of Diomedes to Eurystheus, (9) obtained the girdle (belt) of the queen of the Amazons, (10) stole the cattle of the monster Geryon, (11) stole the golden apples of the Hesperides and (12) captured Cerberus, the three-headed watchdog of Hades.

Jason was a hero of Greek mythology who was the leader of the fabled Argonauts in search of the Golden Fleece. They were called Argonauts because they were sailors in the *Argo*, the great ship. They were a band of about fifty of the most valiant heroes of Greece.

After many daring adventures, the Argonauts arrived at Kolchis. The daughter of the king of Kolchis fell in love with Jason. She helped him capture the Golden Fleece.

Perseus was the son of Zeus and Danae. He was tricked into going after the head of the Gorgon Medusa by King Polydectes. Perseus was helped at his task by Athena, Hermes and the hags of the sea, the Graeae.

Perseus knew if he looked at Medusa's face he would be turned to stone so he used his shield as a mirror and cut off Medusa's head. Next, he freed the beautiful Princess Andromeda and married her. After returning home, he turned King Polydectes to stone by showing him Medusa's head.

GA1310

Atalanta was the daughter of a king in Greece. She was known throughout the land for her swiftness in running. Her father was so proud of her that no one could become her suitor unless he outran her in a foot race. The king decreed that anyone who failed to beat her would be put to death.

Many suitors dared the fate of death in order to gain the beautiful Atalanta but they failed. Finally a handsome young man named Hippomenes won her by using three golden apples. Every time she took the lead, a golden apple rolled in front of her and she stopped to pick it up. When she stopped for the third apple, Hippomenes ran past her and came in first.

The goddess Aphrodite had given Hippomenes the apples and told him how to use them. He and Atalanta became lovers and were grateful to the goddess.

PERSEUS and the HEAD of MEDUSA

Activities

1. There were many other heroes of Greece. There were Cadmus, Europa, Bellerophon and Orpheus. Choose two of them to do a written report on.

2. The Twelve Labors of Heracles are famous throughout Greek mythology. For a special project, study each labor carefully and then attempt to draw and illustrate them all on a piece of poster board. Let your imagination go and really be creative!

3. Where and what was the Golden Fleece?

4. Study the story of Theseus in an encyclopedia and explain how the Aegean Sea got its name.

5. Look up the word *labyrinth* in a dictionary and then explain what this word has to do with the Minotaur in the legend of Theseus.

GA1310

Alexander the Great

Alexander the Great was the king of Macedonia and the eventual conqueror of the known world of his day. He was born in Pella, Macedonia, to Philip of Macedon and Olympias, Princess of Epirus. He often wept that his father, who was a great general in his own right, would do so many great things there would be nothing left for him to do.

Alexander believed in heroes. His mother told him the great Achilles was his ancestor, and his father was descended from Heracles. He was brave and bold in his actions. The great Aristotle was his tutor and from him Alexander began a keen interest in other countries and races of men. From him he also became impressed with the ideals of Greek civilization.

He was nineteen or twenty when he became king. The Greek states didn't like to be under Macedonian rule, and when the rumor spread that Alexander had been killed in the Thracian mountains, Thebes openly revolted. Moving with terrifying speed, Alexander utterly crushed Thebes. Around 30,000 of her people were sold into slavery. The remainder of the Greek states saw the lesson of Thebes and learned.

In 334 B.C. he invaded the Persian empire with an army of 35,000 men. He met the Persians on the banks of the Granicus River and destroyed them with his cavalry. All of Asia Minor was now open to him and the next two years he won victory after victory.

He met the Persian king Darius III in October of 333 B.C. In this battle the Persians lost around 110,000 men. The Macedonians had 4000 wounded and 302 dead. The battle took place at a fortified riverbank near Issus.

Next he went into Egypt. There he founded the city of Alexander. This city became a world center of learning.

In 331 B.C. with 400,000 infantry and 7000 cavalry, Alexander crossed the Euphrates and then the Tigris. At Gaugamela he met Darius for the second time. The Persian army was vast and included elephants, the heavy cavalry of the central Asian steppes, many chariots with scythelike knives stuck in the wheels, Persians, Afghans, Indians and Babylonians. It was a long and terrible battle, but with a charge which he led himself, Alexander won and Darius fled. Babylon surrendered and Alexander captured Susa and Persepolis. The gold and silver treasures of Persepolis were immense and much of this was carried back to Greece.

Alexander married a Persian noblewoman Roxane in 327 B.C. and adopted some Persian customs. He decided to conquer all of central Asia and India. There were many battles with his usual victories. He returned to Babylon where he died in 323 B.C. His body was placed in a golden coffin and eventually taken to Alexandria where it was placed in a magnificent tomb. His son was only an infant and by 311 B.C. his empire split into several sections.

GA1310

57

GA1310

Questions

1. Who was the tutor of Alexander? _____

2. What date did he invade the Persian empire? _____

3. Where did he fight Darius for the second time? _____

4. What happened to most of the great treasures of Persepolis? _____

5. What Persian noblewoman did Alexander marry? _____

Activities

1. Alexander had a beautiful and spirited horse named Bucephalus. In an encyclopedia under "Alexander the Great," read about this magnificent animal and the events surrounding him.

2. Write out a complete history of the city of Alexandria in Egypt.

3. The Battle of Gaugamela (also known as the Battle of Arbela) is considered one of the most decisive battles in history. Write out a detailed description of this battle.

4. There were other philosophers besides Aristotle. Two of the greatest were Socrates and Plato. Write complete reports on both of them.

PLATO

GA1310

Answer Key

Page 16
1. Athens, Rome, Florence, London, New York City
2. Attica
3. Athena
4. Council of elder statesmen
5. Persian Wars
6. Peloponnesian War

Page 17
a. Girl Scouts
b. Statue of Liberty
c. Mt. Rushmore
d. No Smoking
e. Red Cross
f. Caduceus
g. Barber pole
h. American flag
i. American Indian
j. Yang and Yin
k. Eiffel Tower
l. American eagle

Page 18
1. High city
2. Parthenon
3. Pericles
4. Erechtheus
5. Agora

Page 22
1. July 28, 447 B.C.
2. Phidias
3. 228 feet
4. Answers will vary.
5. Doric
6. Might and glory of Athens

Page 31
1. Three—Spartans, Helots, free farmers and craftsmen
2. Spartans were soldier rulers; Helots were slaves; other class performed many tasks and labored in the fields
3. Seven
4. Thirty
5. They were the freest in Greece and participated in many sports in public.
6. Two

Page 37
1. Miltiades
2. The runner who ran to Sparta and back and then ran to Athens and died
3. Athens aided Greek cities in Asia Minor against Persia.
4. King Leonidas
5. Themistocles and the Athenian fleet
6. The Spartan soldiers

Page 45
1. Aphrodite
2. Agamemnon
3. Menelaus, King of Sparta
4. A long narrative poem written in a dignified style that tells a tale of a great hero or tales of several great heroes
5. Hector
6. Ten years

Page 46
1. Heinrich Schliemann, 1870's, Hissarlik, Turkey, the cities of Troy, treasures of gold and silver, proved there was a Troy as the *Iliad* stated
2. Howard Carter, 1922, Valley of Kings in Egypt, great treasure and artifacts, first tomb of a pharaoh that had not been opened since ancient times
3. Hiram Bingham, 1911, 50 miles northwest of Cusco, Peru, on a mountain 8000 feet high, discovered the ruins of an Inca city, an important city almost in tact, could now more fully study the civilization of the Incas
4. Sir Arthur, John Evans, 1900 began the excavation, on the island of Crete, the palace of Minos, most knowledge of pre-Greek Minoan civilization is based on this discovery

Page 47
1. a. golden death mask
   b. gold diadem buried with a princess
   c. gold cup
   d. shield
   e. silver jug
2. a. gold
   b. gold
   c. gold
   d. bronze
   e. silver
3. a. A male, even though a diadem was in the grave. Other items point to its being a male.
4. Answers will vary.

Page 48
1. Odysseus, Athena, Telemachus, Penelope
2. Ten years
3. Athena
4. No one recognizes him, and his wife is besieged by suitors who are eating and drinking at his expense.
5. Telemachus

Page 50
1. 534 B.C.
2. Two obols
3. Each dramatist would present three tragedies and a satyr play.
4. Heroes, myths and legends
5. Large masks, elaborate costumes, elevated boots

Page 58
1. Aristotle
2. 334 B.C.
3. Gaugamela
4. Sent back to Greece
5. Roxane

GA1310

Bibliography

"Athens," *The Great Cities*. New York: Time-Life, 1978, 200 pp.

Barbarian Tides: Time Frame 1500-600 B.C. Alexandria: Time-Life, 1987, 175 pp.

Boardman, John, *Greek Art*. New York: Frederick A. Praeger, 1964, 286 pp.

Bowxa, C.M. *Classical Greece*. New York: Time-Life, 1971, 192 pp.

Clapham, Frances M. (ed.), *Ancient Civilizations*. New York: Warwick Press, 1978, 140 pp.

A Dictionary of Ancient Greek Civilization. London: Metheun & Co. Ltd., 1967, 491 pp.

Durant, Will, *The Life of Ancient Greece*. New York: Simon and Schuster, 1939, 755 pp.

Falls, Joe, *The Boston Marathon*. New York: Macmillan, 1977, 203 pp.

Flaceliere, Robert, *Daily Life in Greece at the Time of Pericles*. New York: Macmillan, 1966, 310 pp.

Glubok, Shirley, *The Art of Ancient Greece*. New York: Atheneum, 1963, 48 pp.

Hutchins, Robert M. (ed.), "Herodotus," *Great Books of the Western World*. Chicago: Encyclopedia Britannica, Inc., 1952, 616 pp.

Levi, Peter, *Atlas of the Greek World*. New York: Facts on File, Inc., 1980, 239 pp.

The Parthenon. New York: Newsweek Book Div., 1973, 172 pp.

Rouse, W.H.D., (Trans), *The Iliad*. New York: Mentor Book, 1938, 309 pp.

_____, (Trans), *The Odyssey*. New York: Mentor Book, 1937, 304 pp.

Sabin, Frances E., *Classical Myths That Live Today*. Chicago: Silver Burdett Co., 1958, 440 pp.

Schaap, Dick, *An Illustrated History of the Olympics*. New York: Alfred A. Knopf, 1975, 388 pp.

GA1310